# THE RECIPE™

Dr. Linda Fuller, Editor.
Wayne Lanford, Book Design & Illustrations
Jeff Relth, Arrowhead Press, Incorporated

# THE RECIPE™ FOR SUCCESS IN NETWORK MARKETING

## A BAKER NETWORK™ PUBLICATION

The founding members of the Baker Network have many years of experience in the network marketing industry. Team members are totally committed to the goals and objectives outlined in the company's Creed and Mission Statement.

### CREED

Free enterprise and the entrepreneurial spirit is what network marketing is all about! May truth and justice about this American way of doing business always be served

### MISSION STATEMENT
TO:

■ Promote, increase, and multiply active participation in network marketing worldwide.

■ Inform the uninformed and re-educate the misinformed. (Network marketing, like the dollar bill, is legal, tender, and private.)

■ Provide the network marketing industry with the best possible tools (books, tapes, brochures, etc.) to achieve their goals.

## ACKNOWLEDGMENTS

A million thanks to special members of the Baker Network - Dr. Linda Fuller, editorial consultant; Wayne Lanford, graphic design specialist; and Jeff Relth, printer extraordinaire. These are team members all doing a little bit more.

Appreciation to wonderful friends for their contribution to the Recipe: Dale, Jo, Jonena, Nikki, Pauline, Roger and Ruth.

An **extra** special thanks to my family - Lorrie, Jonathan, and Tiffany - for their patience.

### *This book is dedicated to them.*

*TO GOD BE THE GLORY!*

# TABLE OF CONTENTS

## SECTION ONE

# THE RECIPE™ FOR SUCCESS

INTRODUCTION ——————————————— 1
LETS TALK A LITTLE ——————————————— 3

## SECTION TWO

# ANDREW'S STORY

CHAPTER 1 ——— HUMBLE BEGINNINGS ——————— 21
CHAPTER 2 ——— SHARE A PIECE OF THE PIE ——— 33
CHAPTER 3 ——— THE RECIPE BOOK ——————— 47
CHAPTER 4 ——— DUPLICATING MAKES IT WORK — 55
CHAPTER 5 ——— PIE PAN GUARANTEES ————— 67
CHAPTER 6 ——— THE FINAL PIECE ————————— 79
EPILOGUE ——————————————— 93

## SECTION THREE

# VALUE-ADDED
### ( EXTRA KEY POINTS )

HOW TO CHOOSE A NETWORK MARKETING COMPANY — 95
SUMMARY OF RECIPE FOR SUCCESS ——————————107

# SECTION 1
## THE RECIPE FOR SUCCESS

### INTRODUCTION

The best way to get your piece of the pie is to help others get theirs! This book is a tool to help others - help others!

Everyone wants - a bigger piece of the pie, financial freedom, to be part of a truly dynamic industry and a no-risk opportunity. Unfortunately, not everyone *has been taught how* to achieve their slice of prosperity. Even worse, many believe it's out of their reach. We're here to change that way of thinking.

*IF YOU GIVE SOMEONE A PIECE OF PIE,*
*YOU FEED THEM FOR THE DAY.*
*IF YOU TEACH THEM HOW TO BAKE A PIE,*
*YOU FEED THEM FOR LIFE!*

This book teaches you how to
# ACHIEVE, BELIEVE, AND SUCCEED !

I magine your success if you had the secret recipe which would enable you to duplicate the golf swing of Jack Nicklaus or Nancy Lopez, the follow-through of Jimmy Connors or Chris Evert. How about the recipe for duplicating the speed and grace of Michael Jordan or gold medalist Jackie Joyner Kersey? What a Super Star you'd be!

The bad news is there is no recipe for duplicating their talents. The good news is there is a duplicatable RECIPE FOR SUCCESS IN BUSINESS that can make you a Super Star in your own right! Even better, once you learn the recipe, you can share the knowledge with others who in turn do the same. Before you know it, you've built a whole organization of Super Stars! Just imagine your success!

This remarkable RECIPE FOR SUCCESS is found in the fictional "rags to riches" story of Andrew, a poor boy who became a billionaire through network marketing. Andrew shares his RECIPE FOR SUCCESS for the first time in this book. By following Andrew's RECIPE you, too, can experience the thrill of success and claim your "piece of the pie"!

## LET'S TALK A LITTLE!

Do you ever talk and dream about "someday" getting your piece of the pie? You know, a better lifestyle, a nicer home, a newer car, vacations, travel, early retirement, true financial freedom? All the nice things you and your family deserve? Well, you can have it - NOW!

This book contains directions on how to obtain your "slice of prosperity." Just learn the proven recipe for success outlined on the following pages and your dreams **CAN** become reality. If you're willing to take the necessary steps to learn this recipe then READ ON, because this book is for you.

Whether you're considering, just beginning or a seasoned veteran in network marketing, this book will help you get BETTER at what you do. The exciting thing about this is you do not have to be SICK to get better. Are you aware that the biggest room in the world today is the "room for improvement?" An important concept, for surely we all have room for improvement!

As you read the chapters in this book and consider the information they contain, it is vital you keep an **open mind.** Some folks have minds that seem permanently fixed and closed. They tend to miss out on a lot of good things life has to offer. Remember, the mind tends to be like a parachute - it works best when it's open!

3

Hopefully, you are one whose mind is open to suggestions and unique ideas (simple in nature but powerful in results). Together we can explore new ways to get **your** slice of prosperity, thereby making the value of this book far greater than its cost. The life that lies ahead of you is yours to live as you wish. Why not seize this opportunity and turn your wishes and dreams into reality today?

I'm sure you've heard of the expression . . .

## K-I-S-S

"Keep It Simple & Succeed." That is the intent of this book - to keep it simple, yet show **you** how to succeed!


## GET WHAT YOU'RE WORTH

Regardless of age or occupation, making enough money is what keeps us all from achieving our dreams, right? The truth is, the only people making money seem to be the Government and Counterfeiters - the rest of us have to EARN it the hard way - more than likely by working for someone else. The problem is if you're working for someone else, you're only being paid 25% of what you're worth. That's just the way it is. Why? Very simply, there are too many fingers dividing up the same pie!

Here is some more discouraging news:

- **58% of all Americans hate their jobs;**
- **85% are dissatisfied with their jobs;**
- **90% earn less than $40,000 per year; and**
- **most teenagers have more spending money than the average retiree!**

In fact, 95% of us will be broke at age 65 except for social security benefits. Imagine working hard 45+ years only to retire on a limited income for the rest of your life?! Do you want some good news? This can be reversed; in other words, work five years, then retire in style. That's more to our liking, isn't it? This book will show you how to do just that!

Andrew Carnegie, the first billionaire in America, once said, "I'd rather have 1% of the efforts of 100 people than to have 100% of my own." An interesting idea, isn't it? The question is, how can this be done?

Some believe the answer might be going into business for themselves. For years, surveys have shown that 90% of all Americans want to own a business, be the boss, control their own financial destiny, and be assured that nobody is going to lay them off. But, 80% still continue to work for someone else.

In his book, ***The E Myth,*** Michael Gerber observes that approximately 650,000 people go into business for themselves every year. Unfortunately, 80% of these businesses fail within five years. ***Do they plan to fail or fail to plan?***

## A NEW PLAN FOR DOING BUSINESS

Now, for the first time ever, you can combine an easy plan (THE RECIPE FOR SUCCESS) with a terrific business opportunity to get your piece of the pie! The key ingredient to your success is the Recipe contained in this book. The business opportunity is network marketing, also known as word-of-mouth marketing or multi-level marketing.

You've been doing this all your life: sharing (not to be confused with selling) your favorite movies, restaurants, products, and services with family and friends. Now imagine earning thousands of dollars for sharing that kind of information. THAT'S NETWORK MARKETING! Combined with the RECIPE FOR SUCCESS, it's as easy as pie to fulfill your dreams.

## THE BENEFITS OF NETWORK MARKETING

Worldwide, network marketing is a $40+ billion a year industry and, like franchising, has been around for more than 30 years.

With word-of-mouth network marketing, U.S. Sprint and MCI have persuaded millions of customers to switch from AT & T to their long-distance service. Multi-million dollar corporations such as Colgate-Palmolive and the Gillette Company distribute specialized product lines and services exclusively through network marketing. Network marketing pays big dividends, and you can bet it won't take much longer for more of corporate America to figure out how they, too, can capitalize on the benefits of this rapidly growing industry.

Word-of-mouth network marketing is cost effective because you pay only for results. Other companies may pay millions to advertise, and then pray for results that may or may not happen.

## DUPLICATING SUCCESS

Network marketing, like franchising, is designed to be an easy way of doing business. You simply DUPLICATE the proven recipe that works - add time, effort, and proper ingredients - and everybody wins! It's just that simple! However, there are differences between the two.

Here are some examples: the average franchise costs between $75,000 and $500,000+. The average network marketing opportunity is less than $100, and with some there is no investment at all! Another BIG difference is that network marketing requires NO employees, NO expensive benefit packages, and NO need to quit your current job.

In network marketing, everyone is independent and works their own hours. However, everyone works closely together because they know and understand the meaning of the word team: T-E-A-M...TOGETHER EVERYONE ACHIEVES MORE. Network marketing is based on the principle Andrew Carnegie lived by: "A lot of people all doing a little."

Amazingly, less than 2% of the American public have been properly informed about this terrific business opportunity. Others, unfortunately have been misinformed and are missing out on their piece of the pie. Well, no more missing out. It's time right now to dispel all of these myths and misunderstandings with the facts.

## MYTHS AND MISCONCEPTIONS

## MYTH NUMBER ONE: "The failure rate for network marketing companies and their distributors is too high."

According to the Small Business Administration and other reliable sources, 90-96% of ALL new businesses in America fail within ten years. Friends, let's not blame the network marketing industry for what is, in fact, a universal problem. Surely that shouldn't stop us from going ahead - it's part of life. Winston Churchill said it so appropriately, "Never give up!"

Robert Schuller (a possibility thinker) shared a great thought, "I'd rather attempt to do great things and fail than attempt to do nothing and succeed!" In many cases, people fail because they **don't work** - it's also called "quitting." For example, we all know people who quit school. Well, school was not the culprit or the problem. QUITTING WAS!

Now, consider this....Some very ambitious distributors  buy a large amount of some type of product, and then "lose" their ambition.  THE PRODUCT IS NOT THE PROBLEM - LOST AMBITION IS!  Distributors can't just sit there and expect good things to happen.  Sitting in a synagogue or a church once a week will no more make you a believer than sitting in a chicken house will make you a chicken! ACTION IS THE KEY!!

## MYTH NUMBER TWO: "There's just too much HYPE and ENTHUSIASM!"

Some critics of network marketing say there's too much hype and enthusiasm.  Can you believe that?? Well, friends, welcome to the real world.  Hype and enthusiasm keep all organizations successful.  Whether it's corporate America, the government, or our churches, everyone depends on hype and enthusiasm to get and keep others interested.

Where would soccer, football and basketball be without the hype and enthusiasm of the cheerleaders? Where would Pop Warner football and Little League baseball be without the cheering, enthusiastic parents on the sidelines?

THINK ABOUT IT!  Hype, enthusiasm, energy, passion, excitement - whatever you call it - is what keeps most of us going. We'll talk more about enthusiasm and its importance a little later.

## MYTH NUMBER THREE: "You'll run out of people."

Interesting, but think about the reality of such a statement. There are about 250,000,000 people in the U.S. and approximately 2% are currently involved in network marketing. Additionally, network marketing takes place all around the world, where there is a total population of more than 5 billion. More people are born in the world every year than are currently involved in network marketing. It's very unlikely that we'll run out of people to work with!

## MYTH NUMBER FOUR: "It's a pyramid; only the ones on top get rich."

We hear this one a lot, and nothing could be further from the truth. In network marketing **everyone** starts at the bottom and works their way to the top (upper crust). Take a look at the cover of this book. THERE'S PLENTY OF ROOM AT THE TOP! Anyone who's willing to work can surpass those who brought them into the business. The possibilities are endless. Think big and think positive!

Only in the church, government, and corporate marketplace is there limited room at the top. Think about it. It's very narrow up there. We're not saying that's bad, but for the very few who do get to the top, if they don't deliver, they're history. CEOs and government officials are under tremendous stress to stay on top. In network marketing, on the other hand, there is plenty of room at the top. Only you, not a boss, voters or a board of directors, control your destiny. THAT'S IMPORTANT!

## MYTH NUMBER FIVE: "Network marketing is illegal."

It is true that pyramid schemes and chain letters, which are interested only in recruiting people and collecting their money, are illegal. However, network marketing is neither of the above. Network marketing is a marketing strategy designed to get **products and services** to the customer. Individual distributors are wholesalers, and earn the commission (profit) which would otherwise go to a retailer.

Network marketing, just like the dollar bill, is legal, tender and private. In fact, many network marketing companies are listed on the New York Stock Exchange. The industry is tightly regulated by the

Federal Trade Commission and the Internal Revenue Service, and is in no way illegal. Period.

## WHAT'S THE DIFFERENCE BETWEEN TRADITIONAL MARKETING AND NETWORK MARKETING?

The objective of marketing is to move a product or service from the manufacturer to the consumer. In network marketing, distributors share their products or services directly with others. They earn, as a commission, the difference between the wholesale and retail prices.

If a retail customer decides to join the network, their distributor sponsors them into the business. The new distributor then becomes a wholesaler who also earns a commission on the difference between the wholesale and retail prices.

The sponsoring distributor may lose a retail customer, but gains much more in return. They receive override commissions on all future orders of the new distributor as well as those of anyone the new distributor sponsors into the network.

The distribution of commissions generally goes four or five levels deep. In other words, "A lot of people all doing a little." **Everyone benefits!** It's similar in some ways to the insurance industry where upper management (those who recruit and train sales agents) get a share of each agent's commissions. Again, the layer of management may be four or five levels deep.

The most traditional way to market and distribute products is through retailing, as is done in stores and shopping malls. Direct sales and tele-marketing are two more widely used techniques. For the newer kids on the block, home shopping on television as well as purchasing via computer link-up have generated sales in the billions.

Sounds great, doesn't it? However, if you want to market your products or services in any of the ways just described, you'd better have millions of dollars to cover the high costs of doing so.

Most entrepreneurs and inventors simply don't have that kind of money, and the smart ones choose network marketing as a viable means of distributing their product or service. Why should they give up ownership to venture capitalists or giant conglomerates who are willing to take a great idea off their hands for a fraction of what it is truly worth!

Thank goodness for network marketing! It offers the entrepreneurs of the world (and those of us who want to control our own destiny) the opportunity needed to succeed!

## WIN-WIN-WIN!

Network marketing is a win-win situation for everyone involved....The consumers, the distributors, and the company ALL WIN! Retailers, wholesalers, jobbers, television networks, and Madison Avenue lose out!

■ WHERE ELSE can you take a product to market with limited capital, pay only for results, price the product competitively by eliminating the middle man, pay distributors 100% of what they're worth and still succeed? NOWHERE!

■ WHERE ELSE can you and I get a piece of that success with little or no financial investment, regardless of age, race, color, creed or educational background? NO WHERE!

■ WHERE ELSE can you build a marketing team of thousands without expensive payroll and benefit packages and get the tax benefits of working out of your own home? NOWHERE!

■ WHERE ELSE can you choose the people you want to work with, choose the product or service you want to share, work your own hours AND retire in one to five years to live comfortably off the residual income from your efforts?  NOWHERE...NOWHERE EXCEPT IN NETWORK MARKETING!

In the Value-Added section of this book we will talk about the importance of what to look for when choosing a network marketing company.  For now let's start moving toward the key ingredient in this book, "THE RECIPE FOR YOUR SUCCESS."

## STEP BY STEP

B elieve it or not, there is a proven technique that can help you turn your dreams into reality.  It's called WRITING THEM DOWN.  It's a fact - the **first step** to reaching your dreams is to write.... them.... down. Otherwise, your dreams are only wishes.  Putting pen to paper and writing out your dreams establishes their importance and crystallizes  them in your mind.  Your servo-mechanism (located in the sub-conscious mind) will then work in harmony with your conscious mind to achieve them.  It really works!

The **second step** to turning dreams into reality is called OUTCOME VISUALIZATION.  In other words, what helps you reach the end result is first mentally visualizing it.  The power of these two steps is absolutely phenomenal!

Many gold medal Olympic champions have said that when they stepped into the winners circle, it was really for the second time.  The first time was in their dreams - visualized and then transformed into a written plan of action.

Take a few minutes right now to write down your dreams - all of them.  You won't be sorry you took the time.  ALL WINNERS DO THIS!

## VISUALIZE YOUR DREAMS

This is not the time to limit yourself.  Be creative, and allow your imagination to work its magic.  Be specific, and include details - A red convertible sports car with leather interior....A luxurious vacation home with windows overlooking the sea, and perhaps some soothing music playing in the background....A trip across the United States in a comfy motor home, visiting historical sites, wonderful museums and fabulous restaurants - and you're all decked out in a new wardrobe.  Do you get the idea?  Now, when you **do** get your piece of the pie, (and you **will,** if you follow the RECIPE FOR SUCCESS!), you'll be prepared to enjoy it.

## A JOURNEY TO SUCCESS

Our journey to success begins with a story about a young man named Andrew.  Andrew was really no different from you and me, except for the fact that he mysteriously came upon a recipe for success in network marketing.  He applied the recipe to his family's product and achieved success far greater than his wildest expectations.  Andrew now shares this RECIPE FOR SUCCESS with you in the following story.

Oh, yes, please allow me a brief, but important, comment before we begin.  You **can** make a great deal of money in network marketing, especially if you follow this recipe.  Unfortunately, based on the amount of money involved, there may be those who think something illegal is going on.

This is amazing, considering that CEOs of large corporations often earn annual salaries in the millions of dollars, and everyone applauds them or looks on with envy. (People seldom question whether anything illegal might be going on there, do they?)

The simple truth is: EVERYONE GETS PAID FOR RESULTS!  If you build a large organization, whether it

is the automobile industry, fast foods, entertainment, or a chain of discount stores, you can earn a large income. If you build a large organization in network marketing, you can also earn a large income. If you write down your dreams and visualize results of earning an extra $500 to $1,000 per month of income, **thats large too!** It's all in the eyes of the visualizer.

You can make the American dream a reality in your life, because free enterprise and the entrepreneurial spirit is what network marketing is all about. May truth and justice about this very American way of doing business always be served. GO FOR THE GOLD!

*Have you but dreamed of wealth untold, but have not quite achieved it...Read and follow what we've prepared, you have only to believe it....*

# SECTION 2
## ANDREW'S STORY

## ANDREW - CHAPTER

## HUMBLE BEGINNINGS

*A*ndrew walked slowly through the garden, stopping to touch and savor the beauty of the roses and the sweet smell of jasmine. He climbed the stairs to the balcony of his palatial home which overlooked the cool calm blue sea. Andrew paused and thought, "Well, grandmother, who would ever have thought that from such humble beginnings I would one day* *have such wealth? I only wish you were here to enjoy it with me." Andrew reflected back to his childhood and could hear his grandmother calling to him as if it were yesterday, "Andrew, come get a nice piece of cherry pie hot from the oven....."*

## ANDREW'S STORY

*About 75 years ago, a young boy named Andrew lived with his grandmother on the poor side of town. Andrew and his grandmother were the only remaining members of a once-large family. They had a truly special relationship and spent time together shopping, playing games and reading books. Andrew loved learning about new things.*

*Several times a month, grandmother would bake Andrew's favorite dessert, a heavenly cherry pie. No matter where he was, Andrew appeared at the table faster than a speeding bullet on those special occasions when he smelled the sweet aroma of cherries and cinnamon.*

*This special pie contained many ingredients required by a young boy to grow up healthy and strong. It was filled with wholesome fresh cherries and special spices that kept those who ate it always wanting more. The pie was absolutely habit forming, but what a nice habit to have!*

*Grandmother told Andrew the pie used to be grandfather's favorite dessert as well. She said that before they were even married grandfather* told her she would be wise to go into the pie baking business. He envisioned a company named "Marie's Pies" or "Pies by Marie." He said she could make a fortune if she did! Grandmother would beam with delight when she talked about how grandfather used to compliment her on her cherry pie.

She knew grandfather was very serious about his compliments, especially the day he wrote these words right across the top of her recipe:  "THIS PIE WILL MAKE YOU HEALTHY, WEALTHY, AND WISE."  He even told grandmother Marie to keep the recipe well-hidden. They both thought seriously about someday doing something with the pie, but other things always seemed to crop up or get in the way. The subject would usually be dropped until the next time grandmother baked that wonderful cherry pie.

Andrew was left alone at age 18 when his grandmother passed away. Without her help, Andrew had to struggle to survive. He missed her loving care and longed for the wonderful cherry pie she had always prepared for him. Unfortunately, there were two important things Andrew had never learned - 1) where the recipe was hidden and 2) how to bake.

*Things got really bad, and Andrew was eventually forced to sell his grandmother's house and most of her belongings in order to make ends meet. One of the last items sold was grandmother's bed. To his amazement, there crumpled between the mattresses was an envelope which contained the secret recipe for grandmother's wonderful pie. Andrew recognized grandfather's handwriting across the top of the recipe, and smiled as he read the words, "THIS PIE WILL MAKE YOU HEALTHY, WEALTHY, AND WISE."*

*Andrew pondered those words for several days. One night while asleep, a voice inside Andrew's head said, "Learn to bake the pie, then sell it. Don't let anything keep you from success. The pie will help keep you healthy, can make you wealthy, and it's a very wise thing to do." "That's it!" cried Andrew. "No more hum-drum life, scrimping and scraping to get by. I'm going to learn how to bake the pie. I will be successful! I know I can do it!"*

*Andrew went right to work making plans and preparing himself for this new venture. He bought a cookbook, pie pans, bowls, spoons, and all the ingredients required to bake pies. Andrew practiced mixing pie crust and fillings, and*

*baked at least a dozen pies using recipes he found in the cookbook. He reasoned that he should learn all he could about baking pies before he attempted grandmother Marie's recipe, and hoped this knowledge would help him be successful.*

　　*Before long, Andrew felt ready. He unfolded the recipe carefully and studied it again, this time at length. Finally, he took a deep breath and began preparing the pie crust and the cherry filling, hoping to duplicate his grandmother's recipe. He placed the pie in the oven and baked it at the temperature and for the time indicated.*

*Although the pie was very tasty, it was not as good as grandmother's. It took Andrew several days of trial and error to perfect the cherry pie. Finally, he succeeded. Andrew could now bake a cherry pie just like grandmother used to make.*

*Thrilled with his success at duplicating the recipe, Andrew quickly realized he would have to do something with his pies if he wanted to become prosperous. Just baking the pie was not enough. Andrew forged ahead. He decided to market his product, calling it "Marie's Pies," after his grandmother.*

*It didn't take him long to discover that most marketing companies have to spend millions of dollars advertising and test marketing a product. He also learned that, despite their well-planned efforts, and spending all that money, they still had to hope and pray for results.*

*Poor Andrew - he certainly didn't have the money needed to market "Marie's Pies" and, even if he did, just waiting for results wasn't his style. Andrew knew ACTION was the key to success, but he was unsure of what action to take. He needed to find a new and creative way to market this wonderful product.*

*Andrew thought and thought. Surely there had to be a more cost-effective way to take his product to market, but what? Andrew was approached by some large companies willing to take the cherry pie off his hands for exclusive rights to the recipe. However, what they offered certainly wouldn't make Andrew wealthy. Besides, this special recipe belonged to his beloved grandmother Marie. Andrew had faith in her pie, and he wasn't about to give it up. He knew that was not the WISE thing to do.*

*Andrew passionately pursued success. He decided to try marketing his product door-to-door. After weeks of making cold calls with only marginal results, he became very frustrated. Andrew always gave more than 100% effort, and couldn't understand why his efforts weren't paying off. He began to feel sorry for himself and to lose faith in his project. Andrew was ready to call it quits!*

**ASK - SEEK - KNOCK**

Remember the promotional pie brochure titled "Here's Your Piece of the Pie," the one that unfolded in your hands and explained how you could turn dreams into reality through network marketing? That flyer was designed to get you to this part of the book.

We may have lost some readers along the way, but that's only natural - some people prefer to merely DREAM about getting their piece of the pie, rather than actually DOING something to get it! It's difficult to help or hold the interest of those unwilling to act.

However, we know you're different because you're still with us. Now, please don't feel sorry for the unfortunate others who closed the book. They've made their choice, and you've made yours. Rather than just wishing, you've taken the first step toward your goal. We're proud of you. You now have the opportunity, just like Andrew, to obtain true financial freedom and turn wishes and dreams into reality.

ASK - SEEK - KNOCK - are three very powerful words which can guide you to success in any endeavor. Well, consider yourself ASKED to consider network marketing. If you are truly SEEKING for the way to get your piece of the pie, there is NO NEED TO KNOCK because the door which can lead you to your slice of prosperity opened when you opened this book!

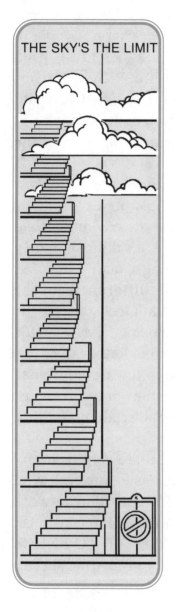

THE SKY'S THE LIMIT

Once through this book, you will understand the secret RECIPE FOR SUCCESS which Andrew received from his grandmother in a most unusual way. But just learning is not enough. Learning must be followed by application. The more you learn and **apply**, the more you will be able to buy!

## STEP UP TO SUCCESS

My friend John Hammond, CEO of the American Motivational Association, coined and trademarked the following phrase: "The elevator to success is out of order - you'll have to take the stairs - one step at a time!" Those words have come to mind often as I worked on this book.

Many times what I really needed was a lift, not more

stairs to climb or steps to take - but I have to admit, my friend John is right. Writing a successful book, or achieving a high position or goal in life is a step-by-step process. BOOKS, POSITIONS AND GOALS DON'T HAVE FUTURES, BUT THE PEOPLE BEHIND THEM DO!

Andrew's first two steps up the ladder of success were learning to bake and making a total commitment to the process. He demonstrated this by investing in the tools required to succeed (pie pans, measuring cups, spoons, etc.).

Likewise, your first two steps up the ladder to success in network marketing are learning to bake (which in this case means learning all about the industry) and then making a total commitment to follow THE RECIPE FOR SUCCESS. The journey of a thousand steps always begins with the first one. If you don't quit, you can get your piece of the pie. So, I'll keep on writing if you'll keep on reading and we'll get to the "upper crust" together. NEVER GIVE UP! KEEP ON CLIMBING!

Andrew, please don't quit...

# ANDREW - CHAPTER

## SHARE A PIECE OF THE PIE

*O*ne evening, after a tiring day of trudging from one house to another with his pies and having little success, Andrew lay on the couch wondering what he could do to change things. He soon fell into a deep sleep, and had a very unusual dream. Andrew's grandmother appeared to him and told him not to be discouraged, not to give up, and to keep faith in himself.

She said, "Andrew, just having the recipe for the pie is not enough to succeed. Your grandfather and I always had the pie recipe. What we lacked was a RECIPE FOR SUCCESS. You must seek and find that recipe to go along

---

*with the recipe for the pie.*

*My dearest grandson, one of the greatest sorrows you will face in your lifetime is to realize how much more you could have accomplished if only you had more FAITH followed by ACTION. Have faith in yourself, Andrew. YOU HAVE THE RECIPE FOR THE PIE. NOW YOU MUST FIND THE RECIPE FOR SUCCESS!"*

*Just before she disappeared, grandmother paused a moment and said, "Andrew, remember when we would go to the bakery shop and the baker would always hand you a cookie? If you liked it we would end up buying a dozen or two. And remember, at the ice cream parlor, how they would give both of us a little taste of the newest ice cream on those tiny wooden sticks? Inevitably, I would end up buying a pint or two to take home and enjoy."*

## THE FIRST PIECE OF THE
## RECIPE FOR SUCCESS

*Andrew, tomorrow bake **two** cherry pies and share them with your friends and neighbors. Watch what happens when you do," grandmother said with a knowing smile. Then she disappeared, and Andrew awoke to his own thoughts. "That's it!" he mused, "In a very mysterious way, grandmother has given me the RECIPE FOR SUCCESS!"*

*The next day Andrew did as grandmother had suggested. He carefully prepared and baked two wonderful cherry pies. He cut each pie into six pieces, and handed out all twelve pieces to his*

friends and neighbors as samples. Everyone remarked about how tasty the pie was.

Later that day, to his surprise and delight, Andrew got orders for six pies from those friends and neighbors. They then shared their pies with guests, who also wanted to enjoy more pie. Within days, Andrew received orders for twelve more pies!

Grandmother's tip was working. Everyone who tasted the pie loved it, and always came back for more. Andrew was convinced now, more than ever, that grandmother had secretly given him the RECIPE FOR SUCCESS. His new company, "Marie's Pies," could not fail!

## GROWING PAINS

*B*efore too long, however, the number of orders began to stabilize and then slowly taper off. This was a natural occurrence - after all, it was only a matter of time before Andrew's immediate circle of friends and neighbors exhausted the number of people with whom they could share the pie. Besides, why should they promote Andrew's product? There was really no reason or motivation to do so.

## THE MISSING PIECE

*A*ndrew was once again in a quandary over what to do.  He was certain there must be some missing ingredient to his recipe for success - but what was it??  A few days later, Andrew sat reading the evening paper.  His eyes got heavy and heavier, and he eventually drifted into a deep sleep.

"Andrew...Andrew, it's grandmother.  I have

something important to share with you.  Listen to me carefully, my dear grandson.  A wise person told me that the secret for success in business is to get a lot of people all doing a little bit more, working together as a team.

"In other words," she said, "it's better to have 1% more effort from 100 people than to have 100% more effort of yourself.  My wise friend calls this the 'Law of the Slight Edge,' and says that whomever learns this law will succeed far beyond their greatest expectations if they have the **right product.**

"My friend suggests you **share the profits** from the pie.  He said this is the missing ingredient to your recipe for success.  This man is very wise, and I know he's right."  Grandmother then said with that knowing smile, "Andrew, share the profits.  Give the people more than a pie.  Reward them as well, and watch what happens when you do!"

Andrew awoke, delighted.  What a tremendous, natural way to succeed - SHARING THE PROFITS!  Grandmother had given him a brilliant idea.  In most companies the profits were shared only with the few at the top.  Consequently, everyone fought to get to the top, just like the kids fought for a place to sit when they played "musical chairs." Many were left with no place to sit, and were out of the game.

Sharing the profits with everyone was totally unheard of, yet that's exactly what grandmother and her wise friend were telling Andrew to do. This extraordinary concept certainly fit with Andrew's way of always looking for new and creative ways of doing things!

Andrew decided to act immediately upon those words of wisdom. He developed a marketing arm of the pie company, which he named the BAKER NETWORK! The primary function of the Baker Network was to educate and promote this new and exciting way of doing business.

Andrew and his marketing team began holding meetings called "Pie Sessions," where he explained to groups of people how they could share in the profits of the pie company.

## SHARING THE WEALTH

People could become associates in the company and earn retail commissions every time they obtained an order. People in the second group who liked the pie could also choose *to become associates and earn commissions every time **they** obtained orders. Additionally, first-level associates would earn commissions from the efforts of the second group, and so on down the line (so coined the term "downline").*

*In other words, things could multiply very quickly. Andrew would explain with the following hypothetical example: If one person sponsored six friends who each sponsored six friends who each sponsored six more friends who purchased and enjoyed the cherry pie, downline commissions would be paid out all along the line. In this illustration, there would be 258 people in the first person's downline, just at the third level. Andrew's company would pay commissions five levels deep.*

*It was amazing how quickly the numbers and everyones commissions multiplied when people worked together with a common purpose and a great product (hence the term multi-level marketing). The beauty of Andrew's plan was that it was so easy!*

*In conversation, an associate would casually ask if anyone knew someone who was looking to get "a piece of the pie". Everyone knew what that meant, because the saying was known and used universally. People always responded positively to opportunities to make more money and fulfill their dreams.*

*"Getting a piece of the pie" had a double meaning in this case, because a wonderful edible product - the cherry pie - really existed! Everyone*

*did know someone who was looking for a better lifestyle - their "piece of the pie" - and everyone loved to eat the cherry pie. Not surprisingly, often the person who was asked was the very one interested. EVERYONE WANTS TO EARN MORE!*

## PAY ME MORE, AND THEN I'LL DO MORE!

Have you ever heard people say, "I'm not going to do any more than I'm paid for! Why should I? If they want me to do more, they'll just have to pay me more first." Many people live by these words, and frequently hear them around the time clock or the water fountain. The truth is, I've uttered them a few times myself.

The problem with this type of thinking is that employers, who are on the other side of the pie (and there always is another side to a piece of pie, no matter how you slice it), are probably saying, "If employees do only what they're paid for and no more, there's no reason to pay them any more for what they do!"

This attitude causes a tug-of-war - them versus us - and the word "we" never crosses anyone's lips. This is a case of team effort in reverse, and is one reason why many businesses do not succeed. How sad!

The simple truth is, no one will pay you more for what you do UNLESS you are first willing to DO more!

It's a "catch-22." That's just the way it is...no if's, and's, or buts about it!

Now read and heed. For you wise ones who are willing to do just a little bit more, extraordinary results can occur. It's even better if you're part of an organization where **everyone** does a little bit more. The results can multiply very quickly, because that's the way network marketing works - everyone doing a little bit more...."The Law of the Slight Edge."

The reason doing a little bit more is so successful is that most people won't make that extra effort. They live in the sea of mediocrity, and do just enough to get by. If you're a person willing to do just a little bit more, to give that extra percent, you will reap financial benefits 10 times greater and maybe even 100 times greater than others who do just enough to get by. You'll pass them by as if they're standing still. Even more exciting, with the extra effort come great rewards.

Here's a good analogy: I used to be a race track fan. You know, I'd "follow" the horses. Eventually I quit because the horses I followed were following the other horses. Way back in the 1961 Kentucky Derby I bet on a horse named Carryback who won the race by a nose at the wire! It was an exciting race to watch, especially if you had a bet on the winner. Although the average race horse back then was worth around $10,000, Carryback's value skyrocketed to over $1 million after winning the Kentucky Derby!

Here's my point:  Was Carryback 100 times better than the average race horse, 50 times better, or twice as good?  The answer in all three cases is **no**, and here's why.  The distance of the Kentucky Derby race is a mile and a quarter long - or, in other terms, 63,360 inches.  On that day in 1961 when Carryback won the race, he

was actually just 1/63,360 better than the other horses.  However, that little bit more made all the difference in the world!

Likewise, if you're willing to do just a little bit more than others, it will make all the difference in your world as well.  You can increase your value 100 times over.  Start NOW to invest that little bit more in your life. BELIEVE IN THE LAW OF THE SLIGHT EDGE!

## MULTIPLY YOUR EFFORTS

D id you know that one penny doubled every day for just one month (31 days) multiplies to over 10 million dollars?  On day 30, it's just over 5 million, while on day 29, it was "only" worth about 2.5 million.

Likewise, a group of motivated distributors utilizing the Law of the Slight Edge can cause things to happen very quickly.  Realistically, in time - one to five years - you could have a downline numbering in the thousands.  The explosive power of multiplying, or doubling, is always at your service.

Let's see how Andrew is progressing...

# ANDREW - CHAPTER

## THE RECIPE BOOK

*A*ndrew reflected on how best to share the information he had acquired. After much deliberation, he wrote a book which he titled **The Recipe for Success**. The purpose of the book was to help associates succeed, and Andrew asked potential associates to read it prior to joining the team.

**The Recipe for Success** *explained, in simple terms, how to succeed using this new way of marketing. Every detail of the marketing plan was covered, and it was written in understandable language. It was like a mistake-proof pie recipe Andrew had once seen in a cookbook.*

*Andrew's recipe for success was based on a lot of people all doing a little bit more, which he termed "The Slight Edge." (He didn't think*

*grandmother's friend would mind.)  It was
designed as a team effort in every way!*

   *Andrew recognized that most people did
not like to speak in public, did not feel
comfortable selling, did not know how to handle
objections or rejections properly, and did not
always have the right answers for the questions
they were asked.  Andrew's recipe for success
eliminated most of the fears and obstacles that
could have kept people from succeeding in his
network.*

   *Andrew asked the school teachers,
association executives, and professional sales
people in the group to handle those types of
responsibilities, because they were generally
more comfortable speaking publicly.  Others in
the group who were perhaps a little shy would be
responsible for greeting guests, preparing
refreshments, setting up the meeting room,
administrative responsibilities, and so on.
Andrew's plan promoted an effective utilization
of the varied talents and skills of all network
members.*

   *Andrew attended to everything which
generally kept people from succeeding.
Associates had only to add a little time, effort,
and enthusiasm for the recipe to work.  Andrew*

always said, "Let the piece of pie and **The Recipe for Success** book do the talking for you! It will get folks interested in attending a Pie Session, where the best presenters on the team can explain our terrific profit-sharing program!"

In **The Recipe for Success**, Andrew cautioned associates about trying to explain the entire program all at once. He believed it might confuse and discourage some of the prospective new associates. His recipe called for two steps prior to attending a Pie Session, but it was twice as effective! People thoroughly understood the business opportunity prior to attending the Pie Session, which gave them freedom to concentrate on learning about the product and the marketing plan. No one was ever overwhelmed with too many facts. The "some will, some won't" philosophy became "more will, less won't." Extra steps, but surely well worth the journey!

## MORE WILL, LESS WON'T!

Another step in Andrew's recipe book called for the building of rapport and friendship with potential customers. It allowed sponsoring *associates to quickly discover if someone was truly interested in the profit-sharing opportunities or only in the actual pie itself. Andrew believed this approach would save everyone a lot of wasted time and frustration.*

*He advised associates to follow the three main steps in the RECIPE FOR SUCCESS, and to always K-I-S-S (Keep It Simple & Succeed!) Just follow steps 1 - 2- 3!*

## ANDREW'S RECIPE FOR SUCCESS
## IN A PIE SHELL

*Step 1:*    *ENTHUSIASTICALLY SHARE A PIECE OF THE PIE WITH OTHERS*

*Step 2:*    *IF THEY LIKE THE PIE (AND MOST EVERYONE WILL) LOAN THEM THE RECIPE FOR SUCCESS BOOK*

*Step 3:*    *INVITE INTERESTED PROSPECTS TO A PIE SESSION TO LEARN HOW THEY, TOO, CAN ENJOY A RICHER, MORE REWARDING LIFESTYLE.*

## LOVE THE PRODUCT

*In addition to the recipe for success, Andrew included other points of information in his book which he believed would support associates in their efforts. For example, to Andrew's way of thinking, success in his business required that associates ENTHUSIASTICALLY LOVE AND BELIEVE IN THE PRODUCT!*

*Andrew acknowledged that associates did not have to be public speakers or sales trainers to succeed, which was helpful and comforting to the less outgoing members of the group. However, he maintained that associates did have to love the product. Andrew advised associates to let their tools (the pie and the book, **The Recipe for Success**) do all the sharing and talking for them.*

*Some people just loved the marketing plan and would become associates right at their very first Pie Session. Where else could someone go "back to school," so to speak, and start earning while they were learning? NOWHERE! It was very exciting!*

*ANDREW'S MISTAKE-PROOF RECIPE FOR SUCCESS COULD PAVE THE WAY TO SUCCESS FOR ALL ASSOCIATES! IT WAS TOTAL TEAMWORK!*

### EASY AS PIE

The beauty of Andrew's recipe was that it really was as easy as pie. All you had to do was hand out sample pieces of the cherry pie to spark an interest, follow up by loaning **The Recipe for Success** book and then, if there was an interest, invite prospects to a Pie Session. Then, "Watch what happens!"

SOME WILL want to take advantage of the opportunities available and SOME WON'T! However, by using our promotional tools (the unfolding paper pie and the recipe book) to interest and educate the public about this wonderful industry, MORE WILL PARTICIPATE AND LESS WON'T!

The point being, if you want to maximize your success in network marketing, you don't have to spend hours talking with prospects about the business opportunity only to discover they are not really interested. You can get this information in a matter of minutes by using the unfolding pie brochure to introduce the idea.

### LOVE THE CUSTOMER

Some individuals might be interested only in the product or service for personal use, and wish nothing beyond being a retail customer. Great! Get samples and sales literature of your product into their hands right away and make them a retail customer. By so doing, you can make a guaranteed profit every time they order.

IMPORTANT NOTICE: If your pie (product or service) is good, people will always come back for more, thereby generating more guaranteed profits. YOU SIMPLY CAN'T LOSE!

## USE THE TOOLS TO YOUR ADVANTAGE

Most network marketing companies produce terrific marketing tools such as tapes, videos and brochures, aimed primarily at selling their products to retail customers. Use them to your advantage. These tools are usually made available at a very reasonable cost, and tend to make retailing a lot easier.

Although these tools do excite your prospects and provide needed product information, they do not usually tend to generate enough enthusiasm or knowledge about **network marketing** as a business opportunity or about the industry as a whole. Without that excitement there is no real motivation to go any further than just being a retail customer.

# ANDREW - CHAPTER

## DUPLICATING MAKES IT WORK

*T*here was no need for Andrew's associate-distributors to sell anything. The word "selling" was taboo in Andrew's book, because he knew most people disliked having to sell anything. Andrew's recipe called merely for people to "share" a piece of the pie and loan out a book. That was it!

Andrew firmly believed sponsoring members should always work for and support their newly sponsored associates by making regular follow-up calls and following through on promises made. This was one of the key factors of the network's success.

"Promise a lot, but always deliver more and then some," Andrew would say. This *philosophy was distinctly different from the traditional corporate structure in which new employees were expected to support the efforts of upper management.*

*Andrew suggested a sponsor supply a new associate with 2 cherry pies (12 pieces) to use as samples to attract new prospects. This type of support by experienced associates was the extra ingredient that helped many a new team member get off to an active and successful start in the business.*

*Plus, giving new associates 12 pieces of pie as a "starter kit" was easily duplicated. Andrew promoted the idea that actions speak louder than words. He believed if sponsoring associates would take care of their downline, new associates would in turn take care of their downline and so on.*

*"That's what duplication is all about," he would say, "and that's how you can build a large organization and earn a large income. Everyone doing their part the right way, over and over again." Andrew would sometimes look at associates with a knowing smile and ask, "Are your actions worth duplicating?"*

*Andrew had developed the perfect business opportunity for everyone! IT COST NOTHING*

*TO START, THERE WERE NO EMPLOYEES TO HIRE, NO EXPENSIVE OVERHEAD AND NO NEED FOR ASSOCIATES TO QUIT THEIR CURRENT JOBS!*

*Everyone was part of the T-E-A-M (Together Everyone Achieves More) concept, and it worked just like grandmother's wise friend said it would (everyone doing a little bit more together). Business was booming because Andrew had finally found the* **cost-effective** *way of marketing grandmother's pie that he had been searching for.*

*Within a short time, Pie Sessions were being held all over the country. At the Pie Sessions, excitement and enthusiasm were the order of the day! The associates with the best presentation skills would present the product and marketing plan in a very professional and enthusiastic way to invited guests, making it easy (as pie) for everyone to build downlines. Duplicating was easy with Andrew's recipe for success.*

## PROSPERITY IS YOURS FOR THE ASKING

The unfolding pie brochure, **The Recipe for Success** book, and the individual who gave them to you are doing everything they can to help you get your slice of prosperity. It's yours for the asking. If you seek to turn dreams into reality and want to earn while you learn, get that caring individual to invite you to a Pie Session ASAP! At the Pie Session you will learn the specifics about **HOW TO SUCCEED** in network marketing.

Some companies call this an opportunity meeting, and it is essentially the same thing. The purpose of a session like this is to give you a "best effort" introduction to 1) the product line or service and 2) the marketing plan (commission structure) in a controlled environment. Let me explain.

Major corporations often spend millions of dollars in a "best effort" attempt to carefully market their products to the public in a controlled environment. Gigantic exhibit halls and convention centers are often used to display their products and services, and only the best presenters give the product presentations. You may be most familiar with the auto and boat trade shows, which are elaborate promotional events.

That's the idea behind the Pie Session (on a much smaller scale, of course) - to present information about the company, its products and the marketing plan in a controlled setting. The Pie Session is educational in nature and professional in format. It is a time for guests to look, listen and learn - and to be assured that the recipe can work for them as well as it works for others!

## BUTTERFLIES IN FORMATION

A n important point I'd like to stress is that not all of us are great public speakers or sales oriented individuals. In fact, according to the **Book of Lists**, the number one fear of all humans is public speaking. Interestingly, the fear of public speaking precedes the fears of financial pressure and of dying.

Surveys also show that when teenagers are asked what they want to be when they grow up, none, we repeat NONE, will say they want to be a salesperson. Yet, for years, people in network marketing have been asked to give speeches and sales presentations in their homes.

Is it any wonder that only 2% of the American public are involved in network marketing opportunities? Too many folks are losing out on some marvelous opportunities as a result of their fears of public speaking and selling.

I've been a student of public speaking for years, and have competed in the World Championship of Public Speaking sponsored by Toastmasters International. I've spoken professionally since 1978 and have presented over a thousand training programs for associations and corporations all over the United States and Canada. Nevertheless, I still get "butterflies" before I speak!

Someone once called me a "model speaker." My head swelled until I read the definition of model: a small imitation of the real thing. The real thing for success in network marketing is duplication, which means being able to make an exact copy.

There is a big difference between modeling and duplicating! Andrew's recipe is simple to duplicate and everyone can succeed.

Those of us in the Baker Network are bothered by the notion that a large part of a person's success in network marketing is based on their ability to sell and speak in public. Sure, we know your upline sponsor will work with you on building a strong presentation.

Unfortunately, that doesn't usually last too long, as they must move on to work with others. Also unfortunately, your fear probably still remains and, unless you have additional support, you may give up your dreams. The Pie Session is intended to provide that needed team support for all associates.

Fortunately for all of us, there are exceptions to the "I don't like public speaking" rule. There **are** associates in every organization who are professional trainers (or seem to be) and have taught their butterflies to "fly in formation." They even **like** the challenge!

Every group has a few of these gifted speakers, the ones you couldn't keep quiet if you wanted to. They do a great job of presenting the product and enjoy doing it. From now on, only those speakers on the team will present the best product (yours) every time. We know this approach will attract many new associates very quickly. It worked for Andrew, and it will work for you.

In time, you will find many qualified presenters and be able to conduct meetings at any number of sites simultaneously. Think about it. The **enthusiasm** and synergy of the group will be multiplied 100 fold! That's difficult to resist, and is one of the powerful ideas behind Andrew's recipe for success!

## FEED THE TROOPS FOR LIFE

I f you **share** a piece of pie with someone, you feed them for the day. If you teach them how to **bake** a pie, you feed them for life. In network marketing, **sharing** a piece of pie is called retailing. Teaching someone to **bake** a pie is called sponsoring...sponsoring is the ultimate goal, as you help others help themselves for a lifetime!

Everyone wants a piece of the pie, but they must have a workable plan of action, one that works easily for them. Andrew's recipe is that type of plan.

The secret for ultimate success in network marketing lies in teaching others how to do it for themselves (duplicating), thereby feeding them for life! What a wonderful purpose in life, teaching others to take off and fly, so to speak, to succeed and enjoy the abundant lifestyle they so richly deserve.

Imagine the satisfaction you'll feel just because you took the time to share an unfolding piece of pie and a recipe book for success with them. Additionally, while you're "sharing and caring" for others, **you**, too, will be prospering and flying high!

Have you ever noticed Canadian geese when they fly south for the winter? I'm sure you have. They always fly in a V formation, and there's a reason for that. Now, think real carefully about that V - have you ever noticed that one side of the V is a little bit longer than the other? There's a reason for that, too! Let me explain.

You see, one side of the V really does have more birds in it. The bird on the point, the lead bird, works very hard on behalf of the flock. It creates a vacuum for those on the left, and on the right it's fighting the head winds.

The geese change positions every few miles; a different bird comes forward to take the lead, and the tired leader falls back to a more protected spot in the V. It has been  both scientifically and aero-dynamically proven that these birds travel 72% farther as a group than one bird can travel fighting it all alone. Those geese are really smart, aren't they? - AND they're helping each other succeed!

Well, what's good for the goose is good for us. People helping each other, everyone doing just a little more to help the whole group. That's the network marketing industry. Birds of a feather flying together!

T-E-A-M !

## YOU'RE IN THE FLOCK - YOUR TURN TO SHARE THE PIE!

With respect to making a commitment to the **growth** of your downline (growth being the only evidence of life or success) you will need to invest in those marketing tools that promote growth. For example, Andrew had the information on his product (the pie recipe), but he needed to invest in the tools necessary to promote the growth of his company. So he did.

Likewise, you will want to invest in tools to promote the growth of your downline. The Baker Network products have been designed specifically for that purpose. You will also need to invest in the informational materials of your chosen company to promote the growth of retail sales. Both types of tools are important in helping you get your piece of the pie. In fact, they are essential if you want to get to the upper crust in network marketing.

Please don't misunderstand the order of importance. The product or service you offer must be good - and consumed - or no income is generated for anyone. In that respect, retailing is a vital element of your success. However, using the company's informational materials to share the product and business opportunity usually produces only consumers. You will want to invest in tools to help you promote the growth of your organization.

By using your own tools of the trade (such as those available through the Baker Network and others) plus the company's informational materials you produce not only a consumer, but a distributor as well. That way...everyone prospers. Welcome to the upper crust!

We advise you to keep a good supply of the unfolding pie brochure and this recipe book on hand to help you support the growth of your business. We believe you can create and double the interest in your business very quickly if you use the pie brochure and the recipe book. We're convinced there are many people who want to know more about the exciting ideas behind network marketing **and** the wonderful opportunities which can help get them started on their way to financial freedom.

The Baker Network materials - promotional pie brochures, books, tapes and videos - will work for you.

They do the talking, the sharing, and the sorting of prospects for you. Although you must sponsor your new distributors and associates, the materials will make it easy as pie! With Andrew's system in place....MORE WILL, LESS WON'T! You're going to love it!

We never again want to hear anyone say, "But, I can't speak in public, I can't sell, and I can't stand prospecting." With this recipe for success in your hands, you'll never have to do those things the old-fashioned way again.

My very special friend and great public speaker, Joel Weldon, has a registered trademark on an 8 ounce can labeled with the words "SUCCESS COMES IN **CANS** NOT IN CANNOTS." You CAN NOW succeed. You've got what you need, and you've got what it takes. No more excuses, please. GO FOR IT! YOU **CAN** DO IT NOW - JUST HAND OUT THE PAPER PIES AND WATCH WHAT HAPPENS!

**P.S.** The person who loaned you this recipe book is sharing their plan of action for success in network marketing because they care about you. It's a straight-forward strategy with no hidden agendas. If you like what you're learning, get yourself invited to a Pie Session. This plan of action will work for you, too!

# ANDREW - CHAPTER

## PIE PAN GUARANTEES

*A*ndrew offered a full money-back guarantee on his pies. He told customers and associates that if (for any reason) they didn't like the pie he would refund their money, no questions asked. He asked only that they bring back the empty pie pan to receive their refund - Andrew called it the "Pie Pan Guarantee."

Andrew offered a second type of guarantee to associates, which he called the "Associates' Pie Pan Guarantee." It was optional, and was available to associates willing to commit 5 or 6 hours per week for just 36 weeks to the three main steps of the Recipe for Success:

**Step 1:** Share at least two pies (just 12 slices) per week with friends and neighbors;

**Step 2:** Loan the Recipe for Success book to those interested in knowing more and

**Step 3:** Invite those interested to a Pie Session.

Andrew's optional Associates' Pie Pan Guarantee stipulated that all money spent on personal consumption of the pie would be refunded to any associate who was not healthier, wealthier, and wiser at the end of the 36 weeks. Period. Why? Andrew knew that it took exactly 36 minutes at 425 degrees to have a successful pie. He also knew that, given the right degree of support and enthusiasm, he could have a successful associate in 36 weeks!

Through his own experience, Andrew knew success was a habit that needed to be formed.

*Repetition was the key to forming good habits, just as it was the key to developing bad ones! Andrew knew that if he could keep associates "hot" on the trail of new habits for just 36 weeks, they would become masters of their own success! No associates who fulfilled their part of the bargain ever lost!*

*One day, Andrew was asked what lucky person in the Baker Network was making the most money. Andrew paused a moment and replied thoughtfully, "Well, the answer is really quite simple - it's the person sharing the most pieces of pie!" He then added that, in his experience, "Luck is that place in the road where preparation and opportunity meet! The harder an associate prepares for opportunities, the 'luckier' they get!" Distributor-associates in Andrew's company generated tremendous amounts of personal income!*

## GROW AND PROSPER

One key to baking a successful pie is knowing how long it takes to bake. Grandmother's pie took 36 minutes at 425 degrees - nothing less would get the desired results. Likewise, nothing less than 5 or 6 hours per week for 36 weeks will get **you** your desired results in network marketing.

It takes time to grow something new and wonderful. Consider, if you will, the moso plant, a member of the bamboo family, found primarily in the Orient. Even one whole year after planting the seed, watering it, and fertilizing with care, there is no sign of growth. Continuous cultivation and care for FIVE years finally results in a moso plant breaking through. Incredibly, once it sprouts, the moso grows at a rate of over two feet per day for six weeks!

This "plant" often reaches heights of over **ninety** feet in just six weeks (plus the five years). How can this be? What in the world happened? It's actually very simple. During that "incubation" period, the moso plant was building a strong foundation underground, so that it could handle its phenomenal growth above the ground!

## BUILD A STRONG FOUNDATION

YOU CAN BUILD A SUCCESSFUL BUSINESS IN NETWORK MARKETING IF YOU ARE WILLING TO COMMIT 36 WEEKS TO DO SO - not 36 minutes, as required for Grandmother's cherry pie, and not 5 years, as for the moso plant - but 36 weeks, 5-6 hours per week. At the end of this time you, like the moso plant, will find that your growth has been phenomenal and that you are UNSTOPPABLE. You will have laid the foundation for a rewarding lifestyle filled with peace of mind which you can enjoy the rest of your life!

Don't cheat yourself! Poet Edgar Guest said it best in his poem titled "The Man in the Glass." Of course, we believe Mr. Guest really wrote it for all of us, but he couldn't find the words to rhyme so he wrote it about just **one** man who is **every** man.

## *The Man in the Glass*

When you get what you want in your struggle for wealth
And the world makes you king for a day;
Just go to the mirror and look at yourself
And see what the Man has to say.

For it isn't your father, mother or wife,
Whose judgment upon you must pass;
But the fellow whose verdict counts most in your life
Is the Man staring back from the glass.

Some people may call you a straight shootin' chum
And say you're a wonderful guy;
But the Man in the glass will say you're a bum
If you can't look him straight in the eye!

He's the fellow to please, never mind all the rest,
For he's with you clear to the end;
And you've passed your most dangerous, difficult test
If the Man in the glass is your friend.

You may fool the whole world, down the pathway of years,
And get pats on the back as you pass;
But your final reward will be heartaches and tears,
If you cheated the Man in the glass!

*- Edgar Guest -*

You **do** have the time to be successful. Everyone can find 5 or 6 hours per week to enrich their lives if they really want to. You have the ability to share your pieces of the pie. You have the right to be on this earth, and to succeed at a level far greater than your expectations. Andrew made a choice, and so can you. Take a good look at the one staring back at you in the mirror and then decide which choices are best for you.

## TURN UP THE EFFORT

Take that first step on the climb to success. "The elevator's out of order, you'll have to take the stairs, one step at a time." Don't cheat yourself. The stairs lead to the upper crust. You can make it to the top in just 36 weeks, especially now that you possess Andrew's recipe.

Will Rogers had a great saying that fits here. He said, "You can't heat an oven with snowballs." Don't heat **your** oven with snowballs. Turn up your temperature to 425 degrees, stay there for 36 weeks, and you'll be "done."

The reason I'm so sure you'll have it made by then is because you will have formed a wonderful new habit - the habit of success! You won't be able to stop succeeding, once you've made the transition. The importance of forming new habits that work may be the best kept secret in life.

People seem content to buy into statements like "No pain, no gain" and "The only place you find success before work is in the dictionary." I surely understand the intent of such sayings and they roll off the tongue pretty easily, but let's face it, pain and work are not most people's favorite things.

Given a choice, most of us tend to find ways to avoid pain and work. Indecision and procrastination, we believe, are intimately tied to the fear of pain and work. By our definition, "work" is something you'd rather not be doing. Ask and look around. Most people hate their jobs, and the last thing they want is more work and pain.

By the way, the word fear broken down by the letters which spell it out - F-E-A-R - means False Evidence Appearing Real.

**Don't let F-E-A-R keep you from your success!**

Unfortunately, this negative kind of talk tends to be depressing and contagious. However, the flip side is that ENTHUSIASM is contagious, too. In fact, whatever attitude one adopts is contagious. So, our advice is to move away from pain and work into fun and profit, because we know that's what you're going to experience in this adventure called network marketing!

Involvement in this industry changes lives. You're not employed by anyone (you call the shots!), yet everyone on the team is pulling for you. It's fun, it's yours, and it's habit forming. It's an amazing thing about habits - we are their slaves. Therefore, why not form good ones and succeed at the same time?

## LIFE CHANGES

About 20 years ago, Jeff, a young network marketing associate, handed me a book that caused me to change the focus of my life. This book, **The Greatest Secret in the World**, was written by Og Mandino. The book incorporates a 45-week plan which challenges readers to replace bad habits with good ones. In my case, it was replace everything or die. I had all the bad habits and was very interested in his concept. I was ripe for the challenge and seized the opportunity!

With the inspiration provided by this book, I finally admitted to myself that I had some significant problems and was going nowhere fast. I came to the realization that a fault recognized is half corrected, and that beginning to solve the problem is half the battle. The journey of a thousand steps begins with the first one. That was it for me! I took the author's advice and started on my 45-week journey, forming new habits, exercising every day, eating the right foods, getting enough rest, and so on.

Mr. Mandino anticipated people might grow disillusioned. He cautioned that the odds of successfully staying with the program for 45 weeks and ultimately changing were against us. However, he made it clear that **if** I was willing to spend the time, GOOD HABITS would be formed. GOOD HABITS - BAD HABITS - it doesn't matter which we choose, we are under their control! Thanks, Og (now a friend and fellow member of the National Speakers' Association) and Jeff (now an associate on our educational staff), for putting me on the right track which helped change my life. Oh, by the way, it worked!

## TIME FOR SUCCESS

Now, I want 36 weeks from you - not 45, just 36! The odds say you won't last that long, but I say you can. The odds may be great, but so are you. You can succeed if you visualize the outcome for your piece of the pie and true financial freedom. No more New Year's resolutions you don't keep. No more dreaming - and wishing - for a bigger piece of the pie. Take a small bite out of life - NOW - and get your piece of SUCCESS!

There will be no stopping you! The beautiful part

about network marketing is that after working for 36 weeks to make your pie, so to speak, the pie then makes YOU. The farmer has to sow new seeds and work hard each and every year to reap a new harvest.

When you share the recipe for success with others who also share it along the way, their success becomes your success. Some people call this residual income - I call it wonderful! If the product is good, the orders will never stop. Oh, yes, one more thing here. If you want more income, all you need do is circulate another pie by sharing it with others, piece by piece!

# ANDREW - CHAPTER

## THE FINAL PIECE

*ithin a few years, Andrew was busy building pie plants all over the country in order to handle the growing demands for Marie's Pies. Andrew was now being called the "Pied Piper of Network Marketing." Other start-up companies were quick to use Andrew's Recipe for Success in building their own organizations. However, they quickly discovered that the real strength of the Recipe for Success is found in the quality of the product. In other words, A GOOD PRODUCT COMBINED WITH THE RECIPE FOR SUCCESS EQUALS SUCCESS IN NETWORK MARKETING!*

*Andrew encouraged all associates to do business with each other, as many of them were* involved in other businesses and endeavors. The contacts and revenues generated in this manner helped bring associates much closer as a group. Andrew also endorsed the notion of doing business with other network marketing companies whose products were of high caliber and whose prices were fair and equitable. "Keep it in the network marketing family," Andrew would say. It was **TOTAL TEAMWORK**, everyone helping each other succeed in every way!

Several times a year Andrew put on a big convention, which he called a "Pie Rally." Associates and prospective associates were invited to attend. People would receive awards for outstanding performances. They would hear and give testimonials about how the company's pie and Andrew's recipe for success had improved their lifestyle.

These were exciting meetings, fun and first class all the way. Everyone got dressed up and enjoyed these galas. The Pie Rallies were big celebrations with wonderful dinners, and of course, dessert was always Andrew's very special pie.

## RETAIL CUSTOMER IS KING

*There were many people who enjoyed Andrew's pie but chose not to become associates in the network, even though there were no fees involved. They were content to remain as retail customers. Andrew always said, "A customer is good for business." Thus, when it came to retail customers, Andrew had two important rules:*

*Rule number 1 - The customer is always right!*
*Rule number 2 - If in doubt, go back to rule number 1!*

*Andrew maintained that retail customers were the "backbone" of the industry, and he advised associates to treat them with special care and consideration. "Someday" he would say, "they may want more than just the pie. They may change their way of thinking and decide they also want a slice of the prosperity the pie can bring them!"*
*Andrew and his marketing team never stopped looking for new and creative ways to benefit the company and its associate-distributors. One of their best ideas was the*

*"Four In One" Thanksgiving Day card. The idea was to send a thank you card to retail customers at Thanksgiving time.*

*It was designed to accomplish four objectives: 1) to THANK them for their continuing business and support and wish them a Happy Thanksgiving; 2) & 3) to also send greetings for a Happy Holiday Season and a Happy New Year; and 4) to extend an open invitation to become an associate of the company. The card was truly unique because few businesses sent Thanksgiving Day cards to their retail customers, whereas everyone sent holiday and New Year's greeting cards.*

*Many retail customers experienced a paradigm shift (change of mind) in their thinking based on that invitation and - joined the team. The team's idea for the Four in One card created Happy Holidays for one and all!*

**IT'S IMPORTANT, SO HERE IT IS ONE MORE TIME!**

**O**ptional Associates' Pie Pan Guarantee: It was and is common practice for companies to stand behind their products with a guarantee. Andrew's company was no exception - any customer or associate who didn't like the product would have their money returned immediately, no questions asked.

As mentioned earlier, it is vital that your associates fall in love with the product or service, whatever it is. The problem is, this often takes time, as in acquiring a taste for a new food or falling in love.

Here's an idea for an optional win-win guarantee program that you can offer new downline **associates** that builds on the notion of the company's moneyback guarantee for customers:  Offer a 36 week "personal use" full money back guarantee. This program is simple-Simon, but will guarantee success for everyone involved.

Under this plan, at the end of 36 weeks, associates who are not totally satisfied with the product or service provided can receive a refund for all "personal use" of the products or services during that period. Generally, the amount will be $25-35 per month for a product or service, and in many cases less than that.

For purposes of illustration, let's say that an associate spends $300 for personal use of the product over a period of 36 weeks (9 months).  That could be your cost to underwrite the guarantee, **but only if the associate keeps his/her part of the agreement.**

In return for the money back guarantee, associates agree to commit 5 or 6 hours per week to apply the three main steps in the RECIPE FOR SUCCESS and to attend Pie Sessions with their guests. If they follow the guidelines to success for 36 weeks and are not satisfied with the product and their new improved lifestyle, their investment in the product is returned, NO QUESTIONS ASKED!

Two conditions negate the optional associates' money back guarantee: 1) if, for any reason, the company distributing the product shuts down or goes out of business (unlikely if the company has been carefully chosen) and 2) if the associates fail to meet their commitment. Everyone wins with this guarantee.

## YOUR INVESTMENT IN TIME:
## BY THE HOURS

### Hour 1:

As an associate, the time you devote each week to getting your "piece of the pie" will be spent in a number of ways. First, you will hand out promotional pie brochures to interested persons who are also looking for a bigger share of the pie. Certainly, it would be foolish to hand out the pies indiscriminately - that would be like planting the moso seed on a dirt road. Remember we reap what we sow! It's important to be wise as you begin building your organization.

For example, you probably wouldn't stand on a

corner handing out the promotional pie brochures to complete strangers, since you would have no way of knowing whether or not they're *hungry* for a richer, more prosperous lifestyle! Instead, a better plan is to tell people about your second job, which is "helping people get their piece of the pie." Then stand back and watch what happens. If someone shows an interest, get their business card or necessary contact information. Then get your tools for success into their hands ASAP. QUALIFY your prospects!

Handing out the pie brochure or giving the extended audio cassette pie version (or both) - in a discriminating way - will likely take less than one hour per week. Handing out six to twelve pieces of the promotional pie brochure per week is a reasonable and attainable goal.

## Hour 2:

A second way that you will use your time is to handle the calls from people who *want to learn the recipe for success,* or perhaps need more information. Isn't it great?? They're calling **you** now, At this point, get **The Recipe for Success** book into their hands, and perhaps pick up your pie brochure and audio cassette pie.

However, you may opt to leave the paper pie brochure with your prospects so they can begin showing it to **their** friends. Remember how people shared Andrew's pie? Well, people will share your pie, too, because it's a tool that generates opportunity, and everybody loves an opportunity!

The pie brochure should have a life span of at least 5 - 10 "bites." That is, if it is retrieved, it can be reused. The same is true of the extended audio cassette pie version, so you are sure to get your money's worth. In these fast-paced times you may want to consider loaning a prospect both the pie brochure and the audio cassette.

Let them read the brochure and listen to the extended audio version - double input. It's simple and...easy as pie! This part of the process will take perhaps one hour per week, leaving three or four hours to go. I say three or four because the next step always varied for Andrew's team, and it probably will for yours, too.

## Hours 3-4:

As mentioned earlier, some people will like the fact you cared enough to share your opportunity and product with them, but will choose not to engage in the business side of things at this time. Your goal at this point would be to claim this contact as a retail customer and thank them for their business. Remember, retail customers are good for business. This step may take 1 - 2 hours per week.

Always leave the "window of opportunity" open, and don't be afraid to use your contacts to further your success. You may wish to ask your new retail customers for the names of any of their friends who might be interested in a lucrative business opportunity. Expect that they will know someone and that they will help you. Remember, you're talking to a satisfied customer. Just ask! This is a simple way to have them help you. In fact, they can simply pass on the paper pie brochure to others. Since every pie brochure has a minimum life span of "5" contacts, you should expect more calls!

People everywhere are hungry for information, but they're *starving* for knowledge. Your "piece of the pie" brochure is **power-packed with knowledge** which just might excite someone enough to "pull the switch" that triggers their interest.

## Hours 5-6:

The final 2 hours of your weekly commitment should be spent attending Pie Sessions with other members of the team and new opportunity seekers. Besides product presentation, time will be spent on "money talk" (the marketing plan) and other topics of particular interest to your group.

This might include new and creative ways to utilize the tools of the the trade, tax-saving ideas, and "pie success stories." There's no need to discuss prospecting, although you might want to make up a list of people you know who may want a piece of the pie, and then send them a pie brochure.

Ah, you will noticed we said Pie Sessions (plural, more than one!) A strategy used by Andrew to increase attendance at Pie Sessions was to *offer a choice of meeting times.* This "alternate choice" strategy is an effective means of gaining a commitment from potential associates.

For our purposes, it would work like this: You could ask a prospect, "Can you come to our meeting on Saturday morning?" and the response might be, "No." Then, you might follow up and ask, "Could you attend a Thursday night meeting?" and the answer could still be "No."

Instead, consider the power of offering a *choice*, as in "We hold meetings on Thursday nights and Saturday mornings. Which would be better for you?" Experts tell us that, nine out of ten times, people will choose one or the other. As so often is the case, the outcome is actually embedded in the presentation! Please trust us on this one. We know it will work for you, and you'll love the results.

There are additional reasons to offer choices of

meeting days. For example, your own busy schedule may occasionally conflict with a meeting, and having the second time available allows you some flexibility. Also, since it's important you attend meetings with your guests, it is more likely you can  make arrangements to fit everyone's schedule.

Another important reason to have two meeting days a week is that it allows more of the best presenters (those who are really comfortable speaking in a group) more opportunities to "do their thing."  By the way, here is an interesting note - research shows that Thursday and Saturday meetings are generally the best for attendance!

Now you have it - the plan on how you're going to spend 5 to 6 hours per week to get your piece of the pie in network marketing!

## THE PLAN FOR SUCCESS

Step 1:      share at least two pies (just 12 slices) per week with friends, neighbors, and others;

Step 2:      loan out the Recipe for Success book to those who request it; and

Step 3:      invite interested persons to a Pie Session.

You can reap so many other benefits as you

succeed in this business!  You'll make new friends whose goals and interests are just like yours; people interested in a more caring, sharing, and prosperous lifestyle.  There will be plenty of opportunities to socialize, play golf, tennis, and share many good times.

Believe us when we say this is a fun business. There's no back stabbing, no pushing, and no shoving to get to the top, because there is no need to do so. Remember - we are a TEAM!  (Please note that the "extra" fun activities listed here, while important and fun, are above and beyond the 5 -6 hours per week you need to commit to your success in this business.)

You are going to fall in love with this industry, just as we have.  There is nothing like it!

## SHOWTIME!

O nce every three to four months, all the teams in your area should have a Pie Rally, where everyone gets together and exchanges stories and information. Associates can share about how their lives have improved as a result of the company's products and the business opportunity of network marketing.  Guest speakers from company headquarters might fly in to address the group and update them on the latest "inside" product information.

It is an informative and fun-packed night! Refreshments may be served, and some teams may even choose to have dinner as part of their rally. What happens is not as important as that it **does** happen! The Pie Rally is a powerful activity, because people have an opportunity to share their successes and feel really good about what they're doing.

The synergism is great! Use your imagination to plan something fun - dress up, interact with peers, laugh, and be "moved" by what this industry - your industry - and your company are doing for you and your team members. This is your night - ENJOY!

## ANDREW - THE EPILOGUE

*veryone who followed Andrew's recipe for success became very wealthy. Their success was a result of their own efforts; their increased prosperity was primarily the result of the residual income paid out every time someone in the group ordered another pie, and they always did! Some associates retired to a terrific lifestyle with peace of mind in less than five years (not the normal 45 years). Everyone lived happily ever after!*

# THE RECIPE FOR SUCCESS IS NOW YOURS

A ndrew's success boiled down to two major ingredients, 1) the product (grandmother's cherry pie) and 2) the marketing plan (the Recipe for Success). Many years later, Andrew was called home to a family reunion, but before leaving on his final journey he passed his RECIPE FOR SUCCESS on to a very special person!

You now hold that RECIPE FOR SUCCESS in your hands. If you are wise, you will take advantage of the opportunity offered you so that you, too, may prosper. Just call the caring person who loaned you this book or the audio cassette version and get yourself invited to an informational Pie Session.

A delicious recipe and words of wisdom shared by a grandmother with her grandson Andrew over 75 years ago created a new way of doing business that is now being done all around the world. Call it network marketing, multi-level marketing, or word-of-mouth marketing. Whatever you choose to call it, however, remember this: IT'S YOUR PIECE OF THE PIE!

## THE END

---

# SECTION 3

## VALUE-ADDED INFORMATION EXTRA KEY POINTS

### HOW TO CHOOSE A NETWORK MARKETING COMPANY

There are many different kinds of "pies" (products) to choose from, everything from A (apple) to Z (zucchini). Your choice of network marketing companies is just as varied. If you don't like zucchini pie, don't eat it!

### FALL IN LOVE

It's important to look for a life-enhancing or life-changing product or service you can fall in love with. Don't rush this decision. If you don't love and use your product, it will be difficult, if not impossible, to generate enthusiasm about it with others.

Some people get up in the morning and try to "psych" themselves up because they've "got to share" an inferior or overpriced product to succeed. Contrast that scenario with those who arise and say, "I've got a great product to share, and I will succeed today!"

## BE WISE

C hoose wisely. Read a company's literature carefully, and check them out. Two great sources of information are the Multi-Level Marketing International Association (MLMIA) and the Direct Selling Association (DSA). MLMIA offers both corporate and individual memberships; DSA offers only corporate memberships.

They're both terrific organizations and have a variety of information available to help you make a wise decision about a network marketing opportunity that will work for you. They both care about the future of the industry, as we're sure you do, especially now that you're considering spending yours with us!

You may have a question about new ("start-up") companies. Making the decision to go with a new company may be a little more risky than selecting one with a history, but it may be the right decision for you. If the company conforms to the letter of the law, has good management and adequate financing, and - if you truly LOVE the product - go for it!  Many times, in the difficulty lies the greater reward!

## THINK PRICE

I t is important to determine that a **company's product or service is not overpriced** for the marketplace.  Overpricing sometimes occurs due to shortsightedness on the part of the network marketing company (who may have assumed distributors wouldn't mind paying a little bit more if they made a little more commission).  Unfortunately, this usually ends in failure for all.

## GENERATING INCOME

W e'd like to restate a very important point:  the **sale of the products or services,** and nothing else, is the primary focus of the best network marketing companies.  Your commissions and the commissions of all those in your downline should be derived from that process.

Other means of making commissions, such as being paid for recruiting others to your downline (some call it "headhunting"), is wrong - in fact, it is illegal - period.  Become a member of MLMIA and check out the companies that interest you. MLMIA will send you a membership/information packet ($5.00 U.S.) which will apply toward your membership.

MLMIA                   DSA
119 Stanford Court      1776 K Street NW
Irvine, CA 92715        Suite 600
(714) 854-5488          Washington, DC 20006
                        (202) 293-5760

EXTRA VALUE:
MLM *SUCCESS*
The Journal for
Network Marketing Leaders
A great monthly read!
1 (800) 927-2527 Ext. MLM

## SUMMARY OF WHAT TO LOOK FOR IN A NETWORK MARKETING COMPANY

❏　　Look for a product or service you can fall in love with.

❏　　Make sure you're not **required** to pay upfront fees or to keep product inventory. Keep your overhead as low as possible.

❏　　Look for a company that pays commissions **only**

❑　Be sure the company offers a fair and equitable guaranteed refund policy on unused product, service, and promotional materials.

❑　Look for a company that promotes and encourages the "TEAM" (Together Everyone Achieves More) concept.

## ALERT !

D o you remember the math formula pi $r^2$ (pie r squared)? Well, unfortunately, there are a few companies in every industry that fit the $r^2$ (ARE SQUARE) business to a "T" - they are squarely fixed on taking care of themselves and no one else. These companies do not project the image of the free enterprise system, and should be avoided like the plague. It is critical that you check out a prospective company.

However, once you find the right company, never let it go! Just apply the recipe - add time, effort, and "the big E."

## THE BIG "E"

To illustrate the big "E," here's one of the Baker Network's favorite stories. We share it to illustrate the importance of a very pertinent ingredient in the recipe for success.

On the first tee shot of the day, a high handicap golfer - a hacker, if you will - hits his drive in the woods and off he goes hunting for his ball. There he finds it, on top of an ant hill. Well, he has a smile on his face from ear to ear because he knows if he took every tee in his pocket and tried to perch that ball up any better he couldn't do it.

So, he grabbed his favorite club, the one iron, and started hacking away, trying to hit the ball. After about ten practice swings (that's what **he** called them) there were only two ants left alive on the hill. One of the ants looked at the other and said, "Mabel, if we're going to get out of this world alive, we had better get on the ball!"

## STAY ON THE BALL

Let me ask you this question...Are you on the ball? The fact that you have this book in your hands and that you have read this far tells me you are. Keep in mind, though, that THE SECRET OF CONTINUOUS SUCCESS IN THE NETWORK MARKETING BUSINESS IS TO **STAY** ON THE BALL!

One of the key elements in achieving this quest is the big "**E**" - ENTHUSIASM for your product. Enthusiasm is derived from the Greek word "entho" which means "God within." Now, that by itself is exciting enough, but take a look at the last four letters of this magical word - I A S M. They stand for I AM SOLD MYSELF. It is absolutely impossible to be truly successful in network marketing (or anything else, for that matter) unless **YOU** are TOTALLY SOLD ON YOUR PRODUCT OR SERVICE.

SECTION 3

---

## ENTHUSIASM MAKES YOU SUCCESSFUL, KEEPS YOU SUCCESSFUL, AND KEEPS YOU ON THE BALL!

Ralph Waldo Emerson made this powerful statement, "Every great and commanding movement in the annals of the world is the triumph of enthusiasm." It's unlikely that anything great was ever achieved without it.

Enthusiasm, as previously stated, is *contagious.* It truly is. Unfortunately, if someone doesn't have enthusiasm, whatever they **do** have is contagious! I think we all know people who can brighten up a room just by leaving it. Stay away from those kinds of people, and whatever you do, don't share your pie brochure with them!

Sometimes associates might ask "But what if I don't always think and feel enthusiastic? What can I do?" Well, the truth is that for hundreds of years, many believed our thoughts controlled our actions. "As a man thinketh, so shall he be." Along comes the great psychologist William James who changes things by saying, "Actions can control your thoughts."

In other words, if you ACT with enthusiasm, you will FEEL and BE enthusiastic. Call it mind control or whatever you like, but the simple fact of the matter is that it works! SO, LOVE YOUR PRODUCT, BE ENTHUSIASTIC AND STAY ON THE BALL BY

## ACTIVELY PROMOTING NETWORK MARKETING AND YOUR PRODUCT!

### RICH ACTIONS

Poor is he who allows his negative thoughts to control his actions. Rich, on the other hand, is he who forces his positive actions to control his thoughts. In truth, your ultimate success in network marketing has nothing to do with your thoughts on how great your products or marketing plan truly are. It really boils down to what you DO with your thoughts and the ACTIONS you take.

The aim of learning is not just knowledge, but action, putting what you have learned to work for you. People who can read and do not are no better off that those who cannot. You are reading right now, but RESULTS will come from the actions which follow. ACTION IS THE KEY TO SUCCESS!

Remember what Will Rogers said? "You can be on the right track and still get run over - if you just sit there." So please don't just sit there. Take advantage of the terrific business opportunities network marketing can offer you, today. Not tomorrow, but today. For tomorrow might never come. Here's what Emerson had to say about this: "Yesterday is already a dream, and tomorrow is only a vision; but **today** well lived makes every yesterday a dream of happiness and every tomorrow a vision of hope." That's **inspiring!**

Word-of-mouth, referral, multi-level, network marketing - whatever you've chosen to call it - is exciting and inspiring too, no question about it. I AM SOLD MYSELF, and hopefully by this time YOU ARE SOLD on it, too! WELCOME ABOARD!!

## OUT OF THE OVEN

O nce you find the right company - product or service - and apply the recipe, in just 36 weeks it will be time to open the oven, so to speak, and feast your eyes on what you have created. It will be beautiful, and it will get even better. You've created a duplicatable propelling force that can only multiply in an upward direction. Just think of all the knowledge you have gained along the way. No one can ever take that away from you. Your part-time earning may now be closing in on your full-time income. There are ten powerful 2-letter words that will have made you a success: IF IT IS TO BE IT IS UP TO ME.

YOU will be responsible for this accomplish-ment. You made the right decision 36 weeks ago. No more being paid just 25% of what you're worth; you're involved in an industry that pays 100%! Within one to five years you should be able to retire in style and live off your residual income. Some might say you were just lucky or say you were in the right place at the right time, but remind them that the harder we work, the luckier we get. Luck is really where opportunity and preparation meet.

## REAPING YOUR REWARDS

Remember all those dreams you had just 36 weeks ago, the ones you wrote down? It's time to get out your list and begin turning some of your dreams into reality - today. Let's go shopping. You've planned for this day, and now it's here. Keep in mind that **not** planning is, in fact, a plan of its own design. When you plan your work, and work your plan, as you have done, it is then time to enjoy the fruits of your labor.

While you're out there shopping for the "finer things life has to offer," remember there are many network marketing companies with great products to offer, too. You can't represent them all, but you **can** use their products and services, thereby helping someone else get their piece of the pie. We can all help one another. That was the premise of Andrew's philosophy of "everyone doing a little bit more."

All of us should help promote the industry which feeds us. Every little bit helps - let's keep the recipe for success in the family of products out there. One snowflake all by itself has no effect whatsoever, but many snowflakes together can bring traffic to a halt and close down a major airport.

There is power in numbers! Let's stay together and build the network marketing industry to new and dizzying heights of success. Turn your dreams into reality by helping others get their piece of the pie TODAY! T-E-A-M - Together Everyone Achieves More!

# SUMMARY OF THE RECIPE FOR SUCCESS
## SIMPLE AS 1-2-3-4

1.  In casual conversation, mention to others that you help individuals get their piece of the pie. Give or loan the unfolding pie brochure and extended audio cassette pie. Do not elaborate (let your tools do their job!) Allow 3 - 5 minutes per contact.

2.  When you receive calls from interested persons (and you will) to learn about the recipe for success, tell the potential associate or customer you'll get the recipe to them right away. Loan the book and/or the audio version of **The Recipe for Success in Network. Marketing**. Some people prefer to read, others may wish to listen, and some will do both (both is best -

double exposure)! Again, each contact will take 3 - 5 minutes plus your travel time to deliver the informational tools.

3.    Invite the now informed and excited prospective new associates to a Pie Session. (Don't forget to ask for your tools back.)  At the Pie Session, prospects will have their first introduction to your product.
The Pie Sessions will be presented by enthusiastic associates who love the product, are committed to the company and network marketing, **and** actually enjoy public speaking.   **There is no speaking and no selling required of you!**  Each team member has a role to play; there is total and appropriate utilization of everyone's talents.

Let the unfolding "Here's Your Piece of the Pie" promotional brochure and **The Recipe for Success** do all the work.  If the product or service is good (like Andrew's cherry pie), you too can be healthy, wealthy, and wise!

## Pie Session Agenda

**1.** Product talk - samples available
**2.** Marketing Plan - $$

**3.** Pie Pan Guarantees (optional)

**4.** Enroll new associates (in **your** downline)

**4.** Encourage new associates to use and enjoy the product! Help them start building their team (Downline) by providing 2 complimentary pies (12 servings) to sow their seeds. Remember, it's duplicatable and - it's inexpensive.

K-I-S-S
KEEP IT SIMPLE
&
SUCCEED!

**P.S.S.** Here's a piece of reality: Not everyone you share your pie with will want to learn the Recipe for Success. That's just a fact of life, and that's okay! Make them a retail customer and ask for a referral! Better yet, let them share the pie brochure and tape with others. They are unique, they're filled with opportunity, and they include your name as the contact person. It's a mistake-proof recipe!

# REFERENCES CITED

Gerber, Michael E.
**The E-Myth: Why Most Business Don't Work
and What to Do About It.**
Cambridge, MA: Ballinger Pub., 1986

Mandino, Og.
**The Greatest Secret in the World.**
New York: F. Fell, 1972.

# PIE BADGES GENERATE INTEREST

GET
"YOUR PIECE
OF
THE PIE"™

ASK
FOR
ONE

Available through the
**BAKER NETWORK**™

## ABOUT THE BAKER AND HIS NETWORK

Len Baker, CSP, also known as the Pie'd Piper of Network Marketing, is a professional trainer,management, marketing, and motivational consultant.

He works with special groups, associations, and corporations across the United States and Canada on mastering techniques that lead to greater production, higher profits, and new plateaus of career satisfaction. He has presented his programs to such companies as AT&T, IBM, NCR, AETNA, Prudential, and USA Today, to name a few.

Len is a long-standing member of the National Speakers Association (NSA) and Toastmasters International. He holds the NSA's Certified Speaking Professional (CSP) designation, an honor of achievement earned through proven speaking experience. In 1980, Len was a top winner in the World Championship of Public Speaking sponsored by Toastmasters.

He is the author of many cassette and video training programs. His born-again experience with network marketing began a love affair with this industry, and he has thought of little else since! Len has spent more than 13 years (a Baker's dozen!) helping those in the corporate setting to achieve their full potential. He has now shifted his focus and vision to helping network marketing companies and their associates/distributors fulfill their dreams.

Len is president of The Baker Network.™

---

## THE PIE'D PIPER™ IN PERSON

Sponsor the Pie'd Piper of Network Marketing at your next meeting. Len Baker will personally present his "HOW TO GET A BIGGER PIECE OF THE PIE" seminar, or "THE RECIPE FOR GREAT LEADERSHIP", how to lead a large organization of entrepreneurs.

For more information and available,
### call: 1 (800) 532-6777

**Duplication** is the key to successful building in Network Marketing. By following a simple **recipe**, duplication is made easy as pie! **PUT THE RECIPE FOR SUCCESS AND ITS SUPPORT TOOLS TO WORK FOR YOU NOW!**

# YOUR TOOLS FOR SUCCESS
## FROM YOUR EDUCATIONAL COMPANY

TOOLS ARE AVAILABLE **INDIVIDUALLY**, BY A **BAKER'S DOZEN**, OR **BAKER'S GROSS** AND BY THE FOLLOWING **TWO SPECIALS:**

| THE "PIE BAKER" INCLUDES: | | THE "PIE'D PIPER" INCLUDES: | |
|---|---|---|---|
| ONE PIE BADGE | Regular $261.00 | 2 PIE BADGES | Regular $522.00 |
| 1 BAKER DOZEN **PIE BROCHURE** | Special $176.00 | 2 BAKER DOZEN **PIE BROCHURE** | Special $297.00 |
| 1 BAKER DOZEN **CASSETTE BROCHURE** | Savings $ 85.00 | 2 BAKER DOZEN **CASSETTE BROCHURE** | Savings $225.00 |
| 3 RECIPE BOOKS 3 RECIPE ALBUMS | | 6 RECIPE BOOKS 6 RECIPE ALBUMS | |

ORDER FOR YOUR TEAM
INVEST IN A BAKER'S DOZEN (13) OR BAKER'S
GROSS (156) AND SAVE MORE DOUGH $ PER UNIT!

# OPPORTUNITY PAGE

| ITEM | QUANTITY | UNIT VALUE | TOTAL |
|---|---|---|---|
| ONE **PIE BADGE** | | @ **$3.00** EA | |
| (13) THIRTEEN (BAKER'S DOZEN) | | @ 2.50 EA | |
| (12 X 13) 156 (BAKER'S GROSS) | | @ 2.00 EA | |
| ONE **PIE BROCHURE** | | PACKS OF 13 ONLY | |
| 1 PACK OF 13 (BAKER'S DOZEN) | | @ **$10.00** EA | |
| 12 PACKS 156 (BAKER'S GROSS) | | @ 8.00 EA | |
| ONE **CASSETTE PIE BROCHURE** | | @ **$10.00** EA | |
| 13 (BAKER'S DOZEN) | | @ 5.00 EA | |
| 156 (BAKER'S GROSS) | | @ 3.50 EA | |
| ONE **RECIPE FOR SUCCESS BOOK** | | @ **$12.00** EA | |
| 13 (BAKER'S DOZEN) | | @ 7.50 EA | |
| 156 (BAKER'S GROSS) | | @ 6.00 EA | |
| ONE **RECIPE FOR SUCCESS BOOK ON SIX AUDIO CASSETTES** | | @ **$49.00** EA | |
| 13 (BAKER'S DOZEN) | | @ 29.00 EA | |
| 156 (BAKER'S GROSS) | | @ 19.00 EA | |
| ★ THE "PIE BAKER" SPECIAL | | @ $176.00 EA | |
| ★ THE "PIE'D PIPER" SPECIAL | | @ $297.00 EA | |
| ONE "HOW TO GET A BIGGER PIECE OF THE PIE" SIX CASSETTE ADVANCED TRAINING PROGRAM | (AVAILABLE SOON) | @ **$79.00** EA | |
| 13 (BAKER'S DOZEN) | | @ 59.00 EA | |
| 156 (BAKER'S GROSS) | | @ 39.00 EA | |
| ONE "**YOUR PIECE OF THE PIE**" VIDEO | (AVAILABLE SOON) | @ **$39.00** EA | |
| 13 (BAKER'S DOZEN) | | @ 29.00 EA | |
| 156 (BAKER'S GROSS) | | @ 19.00 EA | |
| VALUE ADDED VIDEOS, 60 MINS EACH ONE "**INCREASED EARNING IDEAS**" | | @ **$59.00** EA | |
| 13 (BAKER'S DOZEN) | | @ 39.00 EA | |
| 156 (BAKER'S GROSS) | | @ 29.00 EA | |
| ONE "**THE MULTIPLYING FACTOR FOR SUCCESS**" | | @ **$59.00** EA | |
| 13 (BAKER'S DOZEN) | | @ 39.00 EA | |
| 156 (BAKER'S GROSS) | | @ 29.00 EA | |

TRANSFER THIS SUB TOTAL TO THE NEXT PAGE $ [          ]

# OPPORTUNITY PAGE

| | |
|---|---|
| SUB TOTAL **FROM PREVIOUS PAGE** ⟶ | |
| Arizona residents add area Sales Tax ⟶ | |

Within USA:
$3.00 minimum or 5% of the subtotal, whichever is greater.

SHIPPING & ⟶
HANDLING

Outside USA:
$5.00 (u.s.) minimum or 10% of the subtotal, whichever is greater.

**TOTAL** $

(u.s. funds only)

Make check or money order payable to:
**BAKER NETWORK,™ INC.**
3003 N. CENTRAL, SUITE 2208, PHOENIX, AZ 85012

Please check one

☐ Check or money order enclosed.

☐ MasterCard ☐ Visa

Account Number_____-_____-_____ Exp. Date_____

**Card Holder Signature** _____

Please send the items listed to: (No P.O. Boxes please)

Name (PLEASE PRINT) _____
Network Marketing Company:

_____

Street Address _____
City _____ State_____ Zip_____
Phone (___) _____ or (___) _____

FOR MORE INFORMATION PLEASE CALL: (602) 279-6010
For phone orders only, Call 1-800-532-6777
or Fax your credit card order to (602) 279-0110

---

# IT'S DUPLICATABLE!

JUST PHOTOCOPY OR CUT OUT ONE OF THE
FOLLOWING OPPORTUNITY PAGES,
FOR YOUR CONVENIENCE.

**FAX OR MAIL TODAY.**

# KISS
MASTERCARD & VISA ACCEPTED

# OPPORTUNITY PAGE

| ITEM | QUANTITY | UNIT VALUE | TOTAL |
|---|---|---|---|
| ONE **PIE BADGE** | | @ **$3.00** EA | |
| (13) THIRTEEN (BAKER'S DOZEN) | | @ 2.50 EA | |
| (12 X 13) 156 (BAKER'S GROSS) | | @ 2.00 EA | |
| ONE **PIE BROCHURE** | | PACKS OF 13 ONLY | |
| 1 PACK OF 13 (BAKER'S DOZEN) | | @ **$10.00** EA | |
| 12 PACKS 156 (BAKER'S GROSS) | | @ 8.00 EA | |
| ONE **CASSETTE PIE BROCHURE** | | @ **$10.00** EA | |
| 13 (BAKER'S DOZEN) | | @ 5.00 EA | |
| 156 (BAKER'S GROSS) | | @ 3.50 EA | |
| ONE **RECIPE FOR SUCCESS BOOK** | | @ **$12.00** EA | |
| 13 (BAKER'S DOZEN) | | @ 7.50 EA | |
| 156 (BAKER'S GROSS) | | @ 6.00 EA | |
| ONE **RECIPE FOR SUCCESS BOOK ON SIX AUDIO CASSETTES** | | @ **$49.00** EA | |
| 13 (BAKER'S DOZEN) | | @ 29.00 EA | |
| 156 (BAKER'S GROSS) | | @ 19.00 EA | |
| ★ THE "PIE BAKER" SPECIAL | | @ $176.00 EA | |
| ★ THE "PIE'D PIPER" SPECIAL | | @ $297.00 EA | |
| ONE **"HOW TO GET A BIGGER PIECE OF THE PIE" SIX CASSETTE** ADVANCED TRAINING PROGRAM | (AVAILABLE SOON) | @ **$79.00** EA | |
| 13 (BAKER'S DOZEN) | | @ 59.00 EA | |
| 156 (BAKER'S GROSS) | | @ 39.00 EA | |
| ONE **"YOUR PIECE OF THE PIE" VIDEO** | (AVAILABLE SOON) | @ **$39.00** EA | |
| 13 (BAKER'S DOZEN) | | @ 29.00 EA | |
| 156 (BAKER'S GROSS) | | @ 19.00 EA | |
| **VALUE ADDED VIDEOS, 60 MINS EACH** ONE **"INCREASED EARNING IDEAS"** | | @ **$59.00** EA | |
| 13 (BAKER'S DOZEN) | | @ 39.00 EA | |
| 156 (BAKER'S GROSS) | | @ 29.00 EA | |
| ONE **"THE MULTIPLYING FACTOR FOR SUCCESS"** | | @ **$59.00** EA | |
| 13 (BAKER'S DOZEN) | | @ 39.00 EA | |
| 156 (BAKER'S GROSS) | | @ 29.00 EA | |

TRANSFER THIS SUB TOTAL TO THE NEXT PAGE  $ [ ]

# OPPORTUNITY PAGE

| | |
|---|---|
| SUB TOTAL **FROM PREVIOUS PAGE** ⟶ | |
| Arizona residents add area Sales Tax ⟶ | |

Within USA:
$3.00 minimum or 5% of the subtotal, whichever is greater.

SHIPPING & ⟶
HANDLING

Outside USA:
$5.00 (u.s.) minimum or 10% of the subtotal, whichever is greater.

**TOTAL** $

(u.s. funds only)

Make check or money order payable to:
**BAKER NETWORK™, INC.**
3003 N. CENTRAL, SUITE 2208, PHOENIX, AZ 85012

### Please check one

☐ Check or money order enclosed.

☐ MasterCard ☐ Visa

Account Number——  -        -        -        —— Exp. Date ——

**Card Holder Signature** ————————————

### Please send the items listed to: (No P.O. Boxes please)

Name (PLEASE PRINT) ————————————
Network Marketing Company:

————————————

Street Address ————————————
City ———————————— State———— Zip————
Phone ( —— ) ———————— or ( —— ) ————————

FOR MORE INFORMATION PLEASE CALL: (602) 279-6010
For phone orders only, Call 1-800-532-6777
or Fax your credit card order to (602) 279-0110

## OPPORTUNITY PAGE

| ITEM | QUANTITY | UNIT VALUE | TOTAL |
|---|---|---|---|
| ONE **PIE BADGE** | | @ **$3.00** EA | |
| (13) THIRTEEN   (BAKER'S DOZEN) | | @ **2.50** EA | |
| (12 X 13) 156   (BAKER'S GROSS) | | @ **2.00** EA | |
| ONE **PIE BROCHURE** | | PACKS OF 13 ONLY | |
| 1 PACK OF 13   (BAKER'S DOZEN) | | @ **$10.00** EA | |
| 12 PACKS 156   (BAKER'S GROSS) | | @ **8.00** EA | |
| ONE **CASSETTE PIE BROCHURE** | | @ **$10.00** EA | |
| 13   (BAKER'S DOZEN) | | @ **5.00** EA | |
| 156   (BAKER'S GROSS) | | @ **3.50** EA | |
| ONE **RECIPE FOR SUCCESS BOOK** | | @ **$12.00** EA | |
| 13   (BAKER'S DOZEN) | | @ **7.50** EA | |
| 156   (BAKER'S GROSS) | | @ **6.00** EA | |
| ONE **RECIPE FOR SUCCESS BOOK ON SIX AUDIO CASSETTES** | | @ **$49.00** EA | |
| 13   (BAKER'S DOZEN) | | @ **29.00** EA | |
| 156   (BAKER'S GROSS) | | @ **19.00** EA | |
| ★ THE "PIE BAKER"  SPECIAL | | @ **$176.00** EA | |
| ★ THE "PIE'D PIPER"  SPECIAL | | @ **$297.00** EA | |
| ONE **"HOW TO GET A BIGGER PIECE OF THE PIE" SIX CASSETTE** ADVANCED TRAINING PROGRAM | (AVAILABLE SOON) | @ **$79.00** EA | |
| 13   (BAKER'S DOZEN) | | @ **59.00** EA | |
| 156   (BAKER'S GROSS) | | @ **39.00** EA | |
| ONE **"YOUR PIECE OF THE PIE" VIDEO** | (AVAILABLE SOON) | @ **$39.00** EA | |
| 13   (BAKER'S DOZEN) | | @ **29.00** EA | |
| 156   (BAKER'S GROSS) | | @ **19.00** EA | |
| **VALUE ADDED VIDEOS, 60 MINS EACH** ONE **"INCREASED EARNING IDEAS"** | | @ **$59.00** EA | |
| 13   (BAKER'S DOZEN) | | @ **39.00** EA | |
| 156   (BAKER'S GROSS) | | @ **29.00** EA | |
| ONE **"THE MULTIPLYING FACTOR FOR SUCCESS"** | | @ **$59.00** EA | |
| 13   (BAKER'S DOZEN) | | @ **39.00** EA | |
| 156   (BAKER'S GROSS) | | @ **29.00** EA | |

TRANSFER THIS SUB TOTAL TO THE NEXT PAGE  $ ☐

# OPPORTUNITY PAGE

SUB TOTAL **FROM PREVIOUS PAGE** ⟶ [  ]

Arizona residents add area Sales Tax ⟶ [  ]

Within USA:
$3.00 minimum or 5% of the subtotal, whichever is greater.

SHIPPING & ⟶ [  ]
HANDLING

Outside USA:
$5.00 (u.s.) minimum or 10% of the subtotal, whichever is greater.

**TOTAL** [$  ]

(u.s. funds only)

Make check or money order payable to:
**BAKER NETWORK™, INC.**
3003 N. CENTRAL, SUITE 2208, PHOENIX, AZ 85012

### Please check one

☐ Check or money order enclosed.

☐ MasterCard ☐ Visa

Account Number___ - ___ - ___ Exp. Date___

**Card Holder Signature** _____

### Please send the items listed to: (No P.O. Boxes please)

Name (PLEASE PRINT) _____
Network Marketing Company:

_____

Street Address _____
City _____ State___ Zip___
Phone ( __ ) _____ or ( __ ) _____

FOR MORE INFORMATION PLEASE CALL: (602) 279-6010
For phone orders only, Call 1-800-532-6777
**or Fax your credit card order to (602) 279-0110**